Mythical Beasts

MYTHICAL SEA CREATURES

By Joanne Rippin

Cavendish Square

Published in 2023 by Cavendish Square Publishing, LLC
2544 Clinton Street, Buffalo, NY 14224

Originally Published in English by Haynes Publishing under the title: *Mythical Beasts Pocket Manual* © Haynes Publishing 2020

Website: cavendishsq.com

Design and layout by Richard Parsons
Thanks to the following agencies for use of their images:
Alamy; pp 13, 21, 24, 25, 26, 29, 30. **Bridgeman Art Library;** p 6. **Getty**.
Shutterstock; Daniel Eskridge (cover), Grom08 (cover).

Cataloging-in-Publication Data

Names: Rippin, Joanne.
Title: Mythical sea creatures / Joanne Rippin.
Description: New York : Cavendish Square Publishing, 2023. | Series: Mythical beasts | Includes glossary and index.
Identifiers: ISBN 9781502667335 (pbk.) | ISBN 9781502667342 (library bound) | ISBN 9781502667359 (ebook)
Subjects: LCSH: Sea monsters--Juvenile literature. | Animals, Mythical--Juvenile literature. | Mythology--Juvenile literature.
Classification: LCC GR910.R577 2023 | DDC 398.24'54--dc23

CPSIA compliance information: Batch #CWCSQ23: For further information contact Cavendish Square Publishing LLC at 1-877-980-4450.

Printed in the United States of America

The Author

Joanne is an experienced writer and editor, who has published many historical books on a wide variety of subjects. She has a long-standing fascination with mythical creatures, and has a dog who thinks it's half human.

Contents

Hydra

Many-Headed Sea Monster

The world *hydra* means "water serpent" in Greek, but this was no normal snake. It had nine heads—sometimes more, because if one was cut off, several more grew in its place. The most famous hydra in Greek mythology was the child of Echidna and Typhon. It lived in the marshes near the coast of Lerna, in the southern Peloponnese, poisoning the air with its breath and destroying the countryside. Because its parents were gods, one of the Lernean hydra's heads was immortal. Some legends say it had 50 heads, others 100, and others 1,000, but most say nine. The hydra had poisonous breath that smelled disgusting, and its venom was deadly.

HERCULES AND THE LERNEAN HYDRA

Killing the Lernean hydra was one of 12 labors given to Hercules by King Eurystheus. At first, Hercules tried smashing the monster's heads with his club, but each time he thought he had succeeded, another head would grow in its place. In desperation, he called his nephew, Iolaus, to help him. Iolaus came running with burning brands, and this time whenever Hercules severed a head, Iolaus cauterized the stump with fire so a new one couldn't grow in its place. Finally, only the immortal head remained, and once Hercules had severed that with the golden sword lent to him by the goddess Athena, the beast's body died. Hercules buried the still-fighting immortal head under a boulder, where it is said to hiss even now.

Did you know?

It was the goddess Hera who raised the hydra, specifically in order for it to kill Hercules. When instead he killed the hydra, Hera placed it in the sky as a constellation.

OTHER HYDRAS

Another famous hydra is mentioned in the Bible. This hydra is called the Dragon of the Apocalypse and is one of the shapes taken by Satan. It has seven heads and ten horns. Other relatives of the Lernean hydra include many-headed Scylla (see page 24) and the dragon that guarded the golden apples of the Hesperides, both from Greek legends.

The seven-headed Dragon of the Apocalypse is overcome and banished by St. Michael and his angels.

Known Facts

Name: Hydra of Lerna

Family status: Mother was Echidna, father was Typhon

Career: Poisoning people who came close enough and generally causing terror

Personality: Fierce and relentless

Appearance: A huge serpent with many squirming heads

Dangerous marshlands

The gases the hydra gave off were so disgusting that Hercules had to wrap his face in strips of cloth to block them out. The salt marshes where the hydra lived are known for their bad smells—the plants that grow there smell like rotten eggs. Could it be that the legend of the hydra was a way for parents to warn their children not to play near the dangerous waters?

JÖRMUNGANDR
HUGE SEA SERPENT

Before you can understand how huge this sea serpent is, you need to know a bit about how the Norse legends describe their world. The center of the Nordic universe is the enormous world tree, Yggdrasil. Within its trunk, roots, and branches, it holds the nine worlds—some physical, some spiritual. The world of humans (Earth) is called Midgard, and the realm of the gods (Heaven) is called Asgard. Jörmungandr is so immense that he can encircle all of Midgard with his long body and hold his tail in his mouth.

Thor's Fishing Trip

Jörmungandr's bitter enemy is Thor, Norse god of war and son of Odin. One legend tells of a fishing trip Thor went on with a giant named Hymir. When they reached the deepest part of the oceans of Midgard, Hymir warned Thor to reel in his hook because they were close to where Jörmungandr lurked. Thor ignored him and continued to fish until at last he caught something enormous. After a difficult struggle, Thor reeled in his catch. As it came to the surface, they saw the raging, venom-spitting head of the world serpent. Terrified that this might lead to Ragnarök (the end of the world), Hymir panicked and cut the line with his sword, releasing Jörmungandr, who instantly returned to the depths.

Ouroborus

Jörmungandr is an example of an ouroborus. This is an ancient symbol of a snake or serpent in a circle, holding its own tail. The ouroborus symbolizes the cycle of life, death, and rebirth.

THE FINAL BATTLE

Everything in Norse legend about Ragnarök is in the form of a prophecy. It never actually happened in the stories; if it had, we would not be here today. The prophecy says Ragnarök will begin after a period of three winters, with no other season in between, when food and water are so scarce that people begin fighting each other for the scraps that are left. The sun, moon, and stars will disappear, Yggdrasil will shake to its foundations, and the oceans will spill all over the Earth as Jörmungandr releases his tail and surges to the surface of the water. When he reaches land, he will spit his deadly venom over the world. At the same time, his brother, the giant wolf Fenrir, will also escape from his prison and eat everything in his path, including the sun. Finally, Jörmungandr will appear on the battlefield and begin an epic fight with Thor, taking all his power and focus away from his allies. Thor will at last kill the serpent with his mighty hammer but will only be able to take nine steps away from his dead enemy before he drops dead himself from the effects of Jörmungandr's venom.

Known Facts

Name:	Jörmungandr, the Midgard Serpent, the World Serpent
Family status:	Middle son of Loki and Angrboda, brother of Fenrir and Hel
Career:	Thrown into the ocean by Odin; stays in the ocean, holding his tail in his mouth
Personality:	Enraged when disturbed, especially if it's by his enemy, Thor
Appearance:	Gigantic body, long enough to go all the way around the Earth
Symbolizes:	End of the world, the circle of life, rebirth

Did you know?

In Old Norse, the name Jörmungandr means "huge monster."

Kraken

Scandinavian Sea Monster

This mythical beast might actually exist. A giant octopus-like creature, the kraken first appeared in the folktales of Norway and Greenland around 1250 and was still feared by sailors up until the 18th century. It was said to live at the very bottom of the sea, but when it surfaced, it was so large that it could be mistaken for an island. Its huge tentacles were said to be long enough to wrap themselves around an entire ship, which it would then drag beneath the waves, never to be seen again. The kraken was brought brilliantly to life in the Pirates of the Caribbean **movies, in which Davy Jones released it to destroy enemy ships.**

Giant Squid

Giant squid live in the ocean at depths of 1,000 to 2,000 feet (305 to 610 m). Their eyes are the size of soccer balls—the largest of any living animal, and possibly the largest of any animal that has ever lived. Bigger eyes let in what little light filters down to where they live. This helps them spot sperm whales at a distance and give them time to get away before the whales try to eat them. The biggest giant squid we know of was 55 feet (16.7 m)—almost as long as a bowling lane. It's likely this animal is what early sailors knew as the kraken.

Did you know?

The Maelstrom, the world's strongest whirlpool, is in the ocean off the coast of Norway. Early sailors believed the kraken could cause a maelstrom by swimming in circles.

FROM MYTH TO REALITY

During the 17th and 18th centuries, the kraken existed on the border between legend and fact, and it was thought by many seafarers to be a real danger. For example, in 1782, the sudden disappearance of 10 British warships was believed by some to be the result of a kraken attack. In 1857, a Danish naturalist named Japetus Steenstrup found a huge squid beak and, later, other parts of a similar creature, which he believed to be from the same species. He was the scientist who gave the giant squid its name. Following his discovery, around 20 other giant squid were found, but usually only parts of them, and never alive. The first time a live giant squid was photographed was in 2002. As of 2022, live giant squid have only been caught on video twice. Because it is so hard to find and document these animals, there is a lot we still do not know about them.

Known Facts

Name: Kraken

Family status: Thought to be inspired by sightings of giant squid

Career: Pulling ships down to the bottom of the sea, either with its huge tentacles or by swimming quickly to create a maelstrom

Personality: Secretive and hidden

Appearance: Giant octopus-like body, huge eyes, long tentacles with suction cups

The first video

In 2013, marine biologist Richard Ellis filmed the first footage of a giant squid, 10 feet (3 m) long, off the coast of Japan. You can watch this amazing film of a real mythical beast coming to life on YouTube.

MERMAID
HALF WOMAN, HALF FISH

Mermaids appear in the folklore of many cultures worldwide. In European folktales, mermaids—and sometimes mermen—are beautiful sea creatures who, like fairies, have magical and prophetic powers. They have a passion for music. In some stories, mermaid-like creatures called sirens lure humans into the depths with their beautiful singing. Many mermaids around the globe are described as loving ornaments and jewelry, which they often use to decorate their long, shining hair.

The Little Mermaid

This famous Hans Christian Andersen story is about a mermaid who falls in love with a prince she has rescued from a sea wreck. In order to follow her prince on land, she makes a bargain with a sea witch to give up her voice in return for legs. In 1989, Disney made the story into a movie. However, there are differences. For example, in the story, walking was so painful for the mermaid that it felt like she was stepping on knives.

Did you know?

Irish mermaids are called merrows. They have a greenish tint to their skin, webbed fingers, the tail of a fish, and seaweed-green hair. Female merrows are beautiful, but the males are very ugly. Some stories say they can shed their fish skin to walk on land. Mermaids from the Shetlands are called selkies. They are related to mermaids but are half seal rather than half fish, and they can live either in the sea or on land.

Mami Wata

Beautiful, protective, and dangerous all at once, the water spirit Mami Wata (Mother Water) is celebrated throughout much of Africa and the African Atlantic. Mami Wata is often described as a mermaid, with a woman's upper body and the tail of a fish or a snake. Her hair is sometimes described as long and straight, and at other times, curly and combed back. Mami Wata can bring good or bad fortune, depending on her mood. A large snake sometimes accompanies her, wrapping itself around her and laying its head on her chest.

Known Facts

Name: Mermaid

Family status: Half-animal creatures who live in kingdoms beneath the sea

Career: Sit on rocks looking beautiful and combing their hair; some lure humans into the waves

Personality: Sometimes vain, sometimes mischievous or even dangerous

Appearance: Top half human, bottom half usually fish; often wear jewelry and have long hair

Symbols: Combs, shells, mirrors, long hair

Sea creatures

Some say mermaids are based on sightings of animals such as seals, dugongs, and manatees.

NAGA

DIVINE HALF-SERPENT CREATURES

Naga is the Sanskrit word for "snake." Indian nagas are semi-divine creatures—part human, part cobra—who take on different forms. Some are snakes with many heads; some have the head and upper body of a human and the lower body of a snake; others resemble humans with snakes growing from their heads. Nagas can be dangerous to humans but are commanded by Brahma the Hindu creator god to only bite those who are evil. Female nagas are princesses of striking beauty, and some ancient Hindu dynasties claim to be descended from them.

NAGAS OF EARTH, WATER, AND SKY

There are three types of nagas. Earth nagas hide from human sight and guard treasure deep within the Earth. Their underground capital is called Bhogavati. It is a glittering city of flowers and music, ruled by the snake king Takshaka.

Nagas of the water are similar to mermaids. They live in springs, rivers, and lakes and at the bottom of the sea in palaces made of gold, rubies, and emeralds. Heavenly nagas of the sky form clouds and produce rain, but when angered, they devastate the Earth with floods. Heavenly nagas also guard the temples of the gods.

Shesha, king of the nagas

Did you know?

Many successful Bollywood films as well as a TV series have been made about female nagas. In the world of Harry Potter, Voldemort's terrifying and deadly snake is called Nagini. In real life, Nagaland is a state in northeast India, near the border with Burma. The people who live there are called Nagas, although they are not the mythical creatures.

GUARDIAN NAGAS

In Hindu temples in India and in Buddhist temples in Southeast Asia, carvings of nagas are often used outside entrances for protection. The ancient Khmer kings of the country who built the complex claimed to be descended from a banished Hindu prince and the daughter of Shesha, the king of the nagas. His title is "Nagaraja" (*raja* means king). In Tibet, nagas are said to live in underground lakes, where they guard magical gems and precious stones and protect the purity of the water.

This is a carving of Shesha, the Nagaraja, at a temple in Darasuram, India.

Known Facts

Name:	Naga
Family status:	Sometimes all snake, but often half human, half snake
Career:	Elemental guardians of treasure; often live hidden from human view
Personality:	Semi-divine, powerful, splendid and proud, mostly benevolent
Appearance:	Human body and head, snake tail, or a headdress of cobra heads
Symbols:	The cobra, precious gems

Eco-warriors

Nagas are elemental nymphs, which means they are associated with the natural world. Hindu folklore states that if you are unwise enough to pollute somewhere a naga lives, they will take revenge.

Scylla and Charybdis

Sea Monster & Whirlpool Mouth

In Greek mythology, Scylla was a female hybrid creature. She had six necks topped with fearsome human heads. Her mouths gaped wide and were lined with rows of fangs as sharp as sharks' teeth. Below the waist, her body was said to be made up of growling dogs, and it ended in the tail of a fish. Scylla lived in the Strait of Messina in Greece, and any ship that tried to sail through this narrow passage would have to get past her. On the other side of the Strait was Charybdis, a monster whose gaping mouth was a whirlpool, always ready to suck down any ship that managed to escape Scylla.

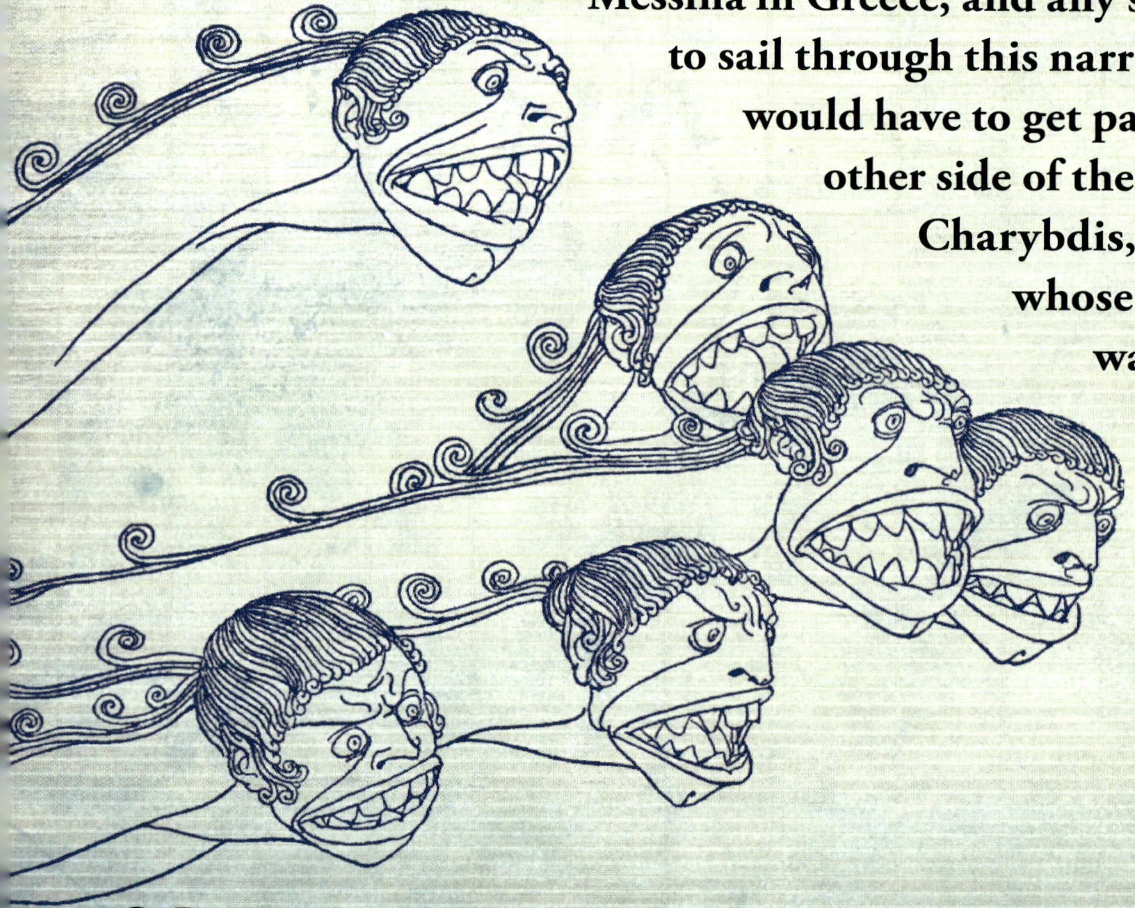

From Nymphs to Beasts

Scylla was once a beautiful sea nymph. Glaucus, a sea god with whom the witch Circe was in love, loved Scylla. Furious with jealousy, Circe transformed Scylla into a hideously ugly sea monster. Charybdis was also once a nymph who was changed into a monster by Zeus as punishment for flooding the land to expand her father Poseidon's kingdom. Scylla would attack ships by snatching sailors from the decks and devouring them. When Odysseus left Circe's island to sail home to Ithaca, the witch advised him to steer closer to Scylla to avoid Charybdis. This was because if he were sucked down by the whirlpool, he would certainly lose his ship, all his men, and his own life, but if he were attacked by Scylla, he might still have enough men left to continue his journey. Odysseus followed her advice. He lost six men, but he and the rest were able to escape.

Circe turns Scylla into a monster to punish Glaucus.

Known Facts

Name:	Scylla, a six-headed hybrid, and Charybdis, a huge whirlpool
Family status:	Both nymphs, daughters of sea gods, transformed into monsters
Career:	Snatching sailors from their ships or pulling them down to their deaths
Personality:	Relentless hunters
Appearance:	Scylla is a strange hybrid; Charybdis has no body, only a mouth
Symbolizes:	A choice between two equally horrible options

Impossible choices

In later centuries, "being between Scylla and Charybdis" became a saying to illustrate an impossible choice between two disastrous options. Similar sayings are "between a rock and a hard place" or "between the devil and the deep blue sea."

SIREN

FEMALE BIRDS WITH HUMAN HEADS

Sirens are often drawn as mermaid-like creatures. However, the three original sirens of Greek myth were far more dangerous, deadly, and disgusting. Usually shown as having the body of a bird and the head of a woman, the sirens lived on land near the ocean. Homer describes them as feeding on human flesh and being surrounded by heaps of rotting bodies. Some sirens had only a human head and neck. Others had the body of a woman too, with just the legs and talons of a bird. All of them, however, had wings.

THE SIRENS' SONG

It was the wings of a siren that made them so dangerous, along with their beautiful singing voices. The sirens lived on a rocky island, and when a ship passed by, their irresistible singing would make sailors so mad with desire to see these creatures that they threw themselves into the water. The sirens would then fly out to the ships and pluck the maddened sailors out of the water, carry them back to their island, and devour them. When Odysseus passed by in his ship, he ordered his men to tie him to the mast so he could hear the sirens' song but resist its power. His men plugged their ears with wax so they couldn't hear it.

Did you know?

It was Odysseus's trick that brought an end to the sirens. They were told that if a sailor ever did hear them sing and live to tell about it, they would die. When Odysseus heard them but couldn't reach them because he was tied to the mast, the sirens threw themselves into the waves and were never seen again.

HARPIES

A similar creature in Greek myth, said to be birds with women's faces, were the harpies. They were children of a sea god, and their names were Aello (storm) and Okypete (swift-flying). Later writers add a third harpy called Kelaino (dark), and Homer talks of a fourth called Podarge (fleet-foot). Harpy means "snatcher," and these sisters were winged monsters—goddesses of the storm winds who swept people away forever.

Known Facts

Name: Sirens

Family status: Some say they were daughters of the river god Achelous

Career: Luring sailors to their death with their singing

Personality: Wild, savage, and treacherous

Appearance: Half bird, half woman

Symbols: The lyre or harp, which some stories said they played as they sang

Friends of Persephone

Some stories say that the sirens began life entirely human. They were companions of Persephone when she was a child, and when she was kidnapped by Hades, her friends searched for her everywhere. They finally begged the gods to give them wings to help them find her.

Glossary

benevolent: Having a desire to do good.

brand: A piece of metal or wood that is used to burn someone or something.

cauterized: Burned with a hot item to destroy body tissue.

devastate: To destroy entirely or nearly entirely.

divine: Like a god.

prophecy: A prediction of the future.

relentless: Showing no lessening of severity, intensity, or strength.

treacherous: Guilty of betrayal or likely to betray.

For More Information

Karst, Ken. *Sea Monsters.* Mankato, MN: Creative Education and Creative Paperbacks, 2021.

AMNH: **www.amnh.org/exhibitions/mythic-creatures/water/sea-monsters**

Index